Bob Chilcott

The Midnight of your Birth

5 CAROLS FOR UPPER VOICES

MUSIC DEPARTMENT

OXFORD
UNIVERSITY PRESS

OXFORD
UNIVERSITY PRESS

Great Clarendon Street, Oxford OX2 6DP,
United Kingdom

Oxford University Press is a department of the University of Oxford.
It furthers the University's objective of excellence in research, scholarship,
and education by publishing worldwide. Oxford is a registered trade mark of
Oxford University Press in the UK and in certain other countries

© Oxford University Press 2017

Bob Chilcott has asserted his right under the Copyright, Designs
and Patents Act, 1988, to be identified as the Composer of these Works

Database right Oxford University Press (maker)

First published 2017

Impression: 5

ISBN 978-0-19-351429-4

Music and text origination by
Katie Johnston
Printed in Great Britain on acid-free paper by
Halstan & Co. Ltd, Amersham, Bucks.

Contents

Composer's note

This collection is made up of five new carols, setting newly-written poems by my friend and collaborator, Charles Bennett. Charles and I have written a number of carols over the past years and I have always enjoyed the way that his poems come in at an angle and paint fresh pictures of certain aspects of the Christmas story. I have always felt that carols need tunes and I have done my best to write some that might stick in the memory, to be sung by upper voices, a sound which I love so much. The dedicatees of these carols include an English junior school choir, two distinguished American children's choirs, a Japanese ladies choir, and adult women singers with a mezzo-soprano soloist. I have, in my mind, though, always wanted this set of songs to share the same feelings of simplicity, freshness, and singability.

for Paul Mayhew Archer and Parkinson's UK, Oxford Branch

The Angel did Fly

Charles Bennett
(b. 1954)

BOB CHILCOTT
(b. 1955)

While you were sleep - ing an an - gel flew_ by, Saw_ you a - lone_ with the

Duration: *c.*4 mins

First performed by Clemmie Franks, Commotio, and Tom Poster in Christ Church Cathedral, Oxford, on 4 December 2016.

Christ - mas, on Christ - mas night.

Christ - mas, on Christ - mas night.

While you were sleep - ing an an - gel flew_ by,

ah_____

for Louise Taylor and the Chamber Choir of Oxford High Junior School

The Blackbird with One White Feather

Charles Bennett
(b. 1954)

BOB CHILCOTT
(b. 1955)

Duration: *c.*2.5 mins

all a-round.   I asked from where his

fea - ther came, he an - swered soft - ly as the rain.   A

black - bird once so long a - go   sang in a land where there

is no snow.   A ba - by slept in a

black - bird's song   out - shone the__ lark._____   It

fell__ as I slept__ like__ pur - est snow,   and brought me a bless-ing from__

long   a - go,_____   a__ bless-ing from__

long   a - go.

for Keiichi Asai, Shizuka Saeki, and the Kyoto Ladies Singers

Kindness
(A raven flew to Bethlehem)

Charles Bennett
(b. 1954)

BOB CHILCOTT
(b. 1955)

Duration: *c*.3.5 mins

When it comes to__ vi - sit, o - pen up__ the__ door.

When it comes to__ vi - sit,____ o - pen up__ the door.

Kind-ness is a bless-ing on us all.'_____

Kind-ness is a bless-ing on us all.'_____

A ra - ven flew_ to__ Beth-le - hem and built a ra-ven's nest with

A ra-ven flew to__ Beth-le - hem and built a ra-ven's nest with

44
straw a wea-ry mo-ther used to take her need-ful rest._____ 'Go

straw a wea-ry__ mo-ther used to take her need-ful rest._____ 'Go

49
home! Go home! You__ bird of night!' said Ma-ry to the thief. The

home! Go home! You__ bird of night!' said Ma-ry to the thief. The

53
S./A.
unis.
in-fant Je-sus mur-mured his be-lief:_____

57
'Kind-ness is a bless-ing,__ kind-ness is a gift.__

No - thing is as rest - ful,___ no - thing is as soft.___

S. When it comes to___ vi - sit,___ o - pen up___ the___ door.

A. When it comes to___ vi - sit,___ o - pen up___ the___ door.

Kind - ness is a bless - ing on us all.'___

Kind - ness is a bless - ing on us all.'___

84 *mf*
qui - et now! You__ dread - ful bird!' said Jo - seph once a - gain. The

mf
qui - et now! You dread - ful bird!' said Jo - seph once a - gain. The

mf
qui - et now! You__ dread - ful bird!' said Jo - seph once a - gain. The

88 **S./A.** *unis.*
in - fant Je - sus qui - et - ly ex - plained:_____

mf

92 *p*
'Kind - ness is a bless - ing,__ kind - ness is a gift.__

p

96
No - thing is as rest - ful,__ no - thing is as soft.__

No-thing is as gen - tle,___ no - thing is as soft.___

No-thing is as gen - tle,___ no - thing is as soft.___

When it comes to__ vi - sit, o-pen up__ the__ door. Kind-ness is a

When it comes to__ vi - sit,___ o-pen up__ the door. Kind-ness is a

rit.   **slower**

unis.   *risoluto*

S./A.

bless-ing on us all,_____ kind-ness is a bless-ing on us all.'

risoluto

Commissioned for the Cleveland Orchestra Children's Chorus
by The Cleveland Orchestra, Music Director Franz Welser-Möst

The Midnight of your Birth

Charles Bennett
(b. 1954)

BOB CHILCOTT
(b. 1955)

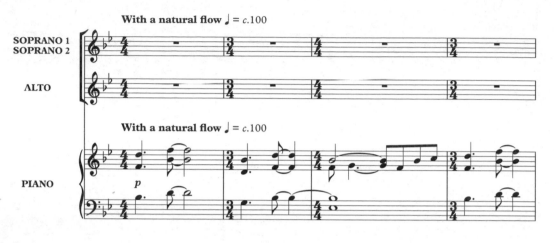

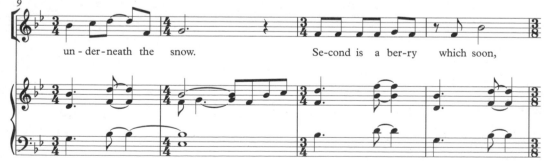

Duration: *c.*3.5 mins

An accompaniment for small orchestra (fl, ob, cl, bsn, hn, str) is available on rental from the publisher's Hire Library or appropriate agent.

soon_ will grow. Third is a ro-bin who comes to_ sing. The

fourth is a blos-som to wel-come, wel - come spring._

S.

Out in the fields_ where the grass_ grows deep, un-der the stars_ we count_

A.

Out in the fields_ where the grass_ grows deep,_ un-der the stars_ we count_

_ our_ sheep, small white clouds that have come to_ earth in the

_ our_ sheep, small white clouds that have come to earth in the

mid-night,   the mid-night of   your   birth.

mid-night,   the mid-night of   your   birth.

The

The

fifth   is   a   fox - cub   play - ing in___ the   sun.   Six is a   sun - set

fifth   is   a   fox - cub   play - ing in___ the   sun.   Six is a   sun - set

un-der the stars__ we count__ our__ sheep,   small white clouds that have

un-der the stars__ we count__ our__ sheep,   small white clouds that have

come to__ earth in the mid - night,   the mid-night of   your__ birth.

come to   earth in the mid - night,   the mid-night of   your__ birth.

The ninth is a tree, a tree for you_ to climb.

Ten is a snail_ who takes, who takes_ his time. E-

-le - ven is a star in the eve - ning_ sky. and twelve is the

ca - rol, the ca - rol of your_ cry._____

ca - rol, the ca - rol of your_ cry._____

for Barbara Berner, Adrienne Broyles, and the St Louis Children's Choirs

The Rain-Tree Carol

Charles Bennett
(b. 1954)

BOB CHILCOTT
(b. 1955)

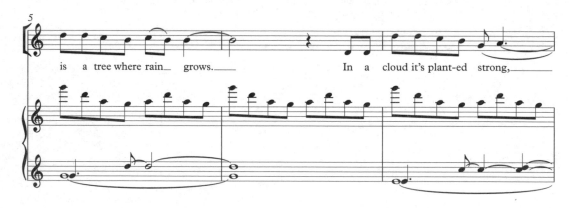

Duration: *c.*3 mins